The Life of

Samuel
Morris

by
Kjersti Hoff Baez

YOUNG READER'S CHRISTIAN LIBRARY

Illustrations by
Ken Save

A BARBOUR BOOK

Samuel Morris

"I WILL BUY YOU BACK, KABOO"

CHAPTER 1

"We meet again, young Kaboo," the enemy chief leered at the young boy. "Your father doesn't seem to be able to keep you in the camp, does he?"

The hot African sun poured heat onto the clearing where the boy was standing. His father, chief of the Kru, glared at the chief of the Grebo tribe who was taunting his son.

The boy met the gaze of his enemy, but his young heart pounded with fear and dread. *Oh, please, Father,* he thought. *Please don't let them take me.*

Chief Kaboo looked down at his namesake. He placed a hand upon the boy's shoulder. "I will buy you back, Kaboo. You'll see. As soon as we are able, we will buy you back."

The chief of the Grebo people stepped forward, his eyes hungry with greed. "You know the terms of our agreement. Every new moon, you must bring us the tribute that you owe us. Make sure you come with full payment. If you fail to pay, it won't go very well for your prince." His harsh laughter filled Kaboo's ears. "Your prince is now a pawn. Again!"

"We will pay!" countered the chief of the Kru tribe. "We will pay." His words were tinged with anger.

"Take him away!" commanded the triumphant African chief. He signalled to one of his warriors. The warrior stepped forward and took the young boy by the arm. As they led him away, the warriors whooped and laughed in triumph.

Kaboo looked back and saw his father standing in the clearing. The young boy's eyes pleaded for help. If only his father could reach out and rescue him! If only his father could take him by the arm and bring him home!

The Kru chief signalled to his son to be brave. The boy was pushed forward. With a heavy heart he

THE YOUNG BOY'S EYES PLEADED FOR HELD

walked away, the distance between his father and himself widening with every step. The warriors and their prize pawn disappeared into the lush foliage of the jungle. The plaintive call of a dove mirrored the harsh loneliness that flooded the heart of the young prisoner. Would he ever see his father again? Would he ever be free from this terrible cycle of suffering?

The warring between the Kru and the Grebo tribes brought much suffering to Kaboo and his family. The treacherous Grebo had ransacked the Kru camp many times, killing the warriors and enslaving those who did not escape into the jungle. The victorious tribe demanded payment to insure peace.

To make sure the Kru would pay, they held the firstborn son as a pawn. Kaboo walked the trail to the Grebo camp. The warriors prodded him with their spears. With every jab, his body shivered with fear. He already knew the cruelty that awaited him. The cold heart of the Grebo chief allowed for no

HE ALREADY KNEW THE CRUELTY THAT AWAITED HIM

mercy toward any slave, especially for the pawned prince.

Despite his fears, the young boy held his head high.

I must be brave, he told himself. *I must be brave for my father. He will buy me back. I know he will.*

At the camp, Kaboo was thrown into a hut where the other slaves were imprisoned. They greeted him in silence, their eyes void of hope. Kaboo closed his eyes and tried to sleep. Outside, the Grebos celebrated their victory with feasting, drinking, and dancing. The rhythm of the drums beat loudly in the ears of Prince Kaboo, drowning out the beating of his lonely heart.

I MUST BE BRAVE, HE TOLD HIMSELF

"YOU INSULT ME WITH THIS MEAGER PAYMENT!"

CHAPTER 2

"It is not enough!" scoffed the Grebo chief. "You must bring me more!"

Kaboo's father and his people had brought the first payment toward buying back their prince. They had labored hard to gather baskets of palm kernels, chunks of dried rubber, and a few pieces of ivory to place at the feet of their enemy. To their dismay, the Grebo chief shook his head and laughed at their offering.

"You insult me with this meager payment," said the chief. "Can it be that you are too lazy to work for the young prince?" He pointed to Kaboo who stood at the edge of the clearing, two warriors on either side of him.

Kaboo's hopes for freedom crumpled beneath the scornful laughter of the Grebo chief. The boy stood straight and tall, despite the weariness with which his muscles ached. The Grebos forced Kaboo to work from the first trace of dawn until darkness fell. But for his father's sake and for the honor of his tribe, Kaboo would let no sign of strain betray his tiredness or his fears.

The chief of the Kru looked at his son, his eyes filled with longing. He knew many new moons would come and go before he would be able to pay off the Grebos.

"I am weary of your presence," snapped the Grebo chief. "Go back to your camp." His dark eyes glistened in the afternoon sun. "See to it that your people work harder," he hissed. "Perhaps I shall have to provide you with some incentive." He threw back his head and laughed. His warriors brandished their spears at Kaboo and joined their voices with the laughter of their chief.

Chief Kaboo turned away, signalling his men to follow. Once again young Kaboo felt the pain of

"GO BACK TO YOUR CAMP!"

separation tear at his heart. The bonds of slavery tightened around his mind, freezing all thought of freedom.

Suddenly, the drums in the camps began to beat, slowly, with a taunting rhythm. Kaboo's blood ran cold. He watched as the chief gave a signal to his men. The other slaves were brought into the clearing. One of the guards grabbed Kaboo and led him to a tree at the edge of the camp. Using a rough, thick piece of vine, they quickly tied the young prince to the tree.

The Grebo chief drank deeply from a nearby pot of rum. He laughed long and hard. The drums beat faster. Grabbing a thorny vine from the hands of an assistant, the chief leaned down to whisper in his captive's ear, "I hope this will inspire your father to pay us in full." He waved the vine in front of Kaboo's face.

The young boy gritted his teeth. *Be brave*, he said

THEY TIED THE YOUNG PRINCE TO A TREE

to himself. *Be brave.*

The chief laughed again and nodded to the drummers. The hands of the drummers became a blur and the rhythm reached a feverish pitch.

The chief raised the thick vine over his head and let out a piercing scream. With all his might, he brought down the whip across the young boy's soft ebony back. The poisonous thorns tore open Kaboo's flesh in streaks of pain. Again and again, the chief whipped the boy.

The Grebos laughed and shrieked at the sight of their pawn's torture. They danced around the camp, mimicking the beating, pulling down imaginary whips, and laughing gleefully.

Kaboo endured the pain as best he could. He fought the urge to scream. The intense pain forced involuntary tears to slip silently down his cheeks. Finally the chief held the whip still. He turned to the horrified Kru slaves who had been forced to watch

KABOO ENDURED THE PAIN AS BEST HE COULD

their prince's torture. He pointed to one of the slaves. The young woman was pushed forward. She stood trembling before the dreaded chief.

"Go back to your camp. Tell Chief Kaboo and your people what you have seen with your own eyes." He flicked the vine toward the bleeding pawn. "This is how your prince will be treated until you pay his ransom in full. Now go!" he commanded.

The woman dashed out of the camp and disappeared down the trail. Kaboo was untied and secured inside the prisoner's hut. His back burned with pain. The poison from the thorns infected his blood, causing chills and fever. For the moment, the terrible physical pain crowded out the agony of his tortured soul.

"THIS IS HOW YOUR PRINCE WILL BE TREATED..."

SEVERAL NEW MOONS HAD COME AND GONE

The noisy chatter of the pepper bird greeted the rising sun and awakened Kaboo from his sleep. He shifted painfully to his side. The open cuts on his back and legs were caked with dried blood. The fiery red tentacles of infection criss-crossed his skin. Breathing burned his chest.

The boy trailed his finger slowly in the dusty smoothness of the hard-packed dirt floor. Several new moons had come and gone. With each passing month, Kaboo's hopes for freedom had dwindled. The offerings his father presented to the greedy Grebo chief were never satisfactory.

With each failed visit, the enemy chief poured out his wrath on young Kaboo. His body was covered with open sores and burns from the whippings.

Kaboo sighed. He was kept isolated from the other slaves. The loneliness and lack of love was more than he could bear. The customary lucky charms of his people that he wore around his neck and ankles had long since been stripped from him. They had not protected him from harm, anyway. His body was gravely weakened by what had become daily torture.

A sudden noisy commotion in the camp pulled Kaboo's head from the floor. Dogs barked wildly. Young children shouted and jeered the visitors.

"Father," whispered Kaboo.

Two warriors burst into Kaboo's hut. They jerked him roughly to his feet. Kaboo was escorted to the center of the clearing. His heart raced at seeing the face of his father.

In the clearing, Chief Kaboo and his people placed baskets of rice at the feet of the Grebo chief. The harvest had been plentiful. Surely this time it was enough! Kaboo looked eagerly to watch the response of the Grebo chief.

"FATHER", WHISPERED KABOO

SAMUEL MORRIS

"You must be joking," snarled the chief. He reached out with his foot and kicked one of the baskets over. "This is hardly a tribute worthy of such a great and mighty warrior as I!"

The Grebos shouted in agreement with their chief. Kaboo's father stepped forward and stared determinedly into his enemy's eyes.

"I assumed you were going to respond unfavorably to our generous offering," he said boldly. "Therefore I have another offer to make."

The Grebo chief leaned forward, his eyes glinting with greed.

"What is it?" he demanded.

Chief Kaboo signalled to one of the Kru. One of the women came forth from the group, leading a little girl by the hand. Kaboo sucked in his breath.

Little One! Kaboo stared with longing at his sister. The sight of her chubby cheeks and sweet brown eyes overwhelmed Kaboo with feelings of

"...I HAVE ANOTHER OFFER TO MAKE"

love and longing. The little girl looked around the camp, bewildered. She was too frightened to cry.

"This is my daughter," Chief Kaboo announced. "Take her as a pawn and give me back my son. We will then pay the balance of the ransom as soon as we can."

The Grebo chief shook his head in disbelief. "Your daughter? You are offering me a worthless female child?"

He threw back his head and began to laugh. His cruel laughter slapped across Kaboo's heart like a whip.

"You must take my daughter!" insisted Chief Kaboo. "My people need their prince. You have kept him long enough. Be reasonable."

To the surprise of everyone, young Kaboo stepped forward.

"No, Father, no," begged Kaboo. "Do not do this thing. I am a prince. I can bear this torture much

"NO, FATHER, NO... DO NOT DO THIS THING"

better than my sister could. Please, do not offer her. I am strong. I can do it."

All eyes were on young Kaboo. His father looked at his son, his heart breaking at the sight of his brave young face.

"That's very noble of you," jeered the Grebo chief, "but I would never accept this ridiculous offer." He turned his attention to Kaboo's father. "Your daughter has no worth! You are desperate! Only cowards and fools wear their desperation on their faces. Get out! And next month you had better not fail to please me." He looked menacingly at his pawn. "You had better not fail," he repeated.

Kaboo's father turned away. One of the women picked up Little One and followed quickly after her people. Young Kaboo was dragged to the field to work. By noon, the chief was drunk, his anger over the latest offer fueled by the rum. He ordered Kaboo brought to the whipping tree. The boy was beaten

"I AM STRONG...I CAN DO IT"

until he passed out. Another Kru slave was released.

"Tell your chief that's what I think about his stupid offer!" shouted the chief after the fleeing slave. His words were slurred. "Tell him his precious son is paying for his father's foolishness."

When Kaboo came to, he found himself on the ground of the hut. His strength had drained away. Bleeding and infection were drawing the life from his young body. All hope drained from him as he lay on the floor.

I'm going to die, he thought. He remembered what he had been taught about the spirits that lived in the water and trees and stones. They had not helped him to escape his suffering. Thoughts of death terrified him.

What happens to you when you die? the boy wondered. In his short life, he had seen a lot of death. Young children and old people dying from illness, young men killed by their enemies. It was always the

"HIS SON IS PAYING FOR HIS FATHER'S FOOLISHNESS"

same. Life disappeared. The person was cut off from those who knew him. Was there only endless darkness after death? Did death stretch on forever like a black river of separation and nothingness?

The next two days blended into a painful blur of fierce whippings. The young Kru prince could no longer stand and had to be tied to the tree. Two logs were tied together in criss-cross fashion. They draped the boy over the crossed wood so the beatings could continue.

Kaboo was dying. The fear of death no longer mattered. He only wanted release from the relentless suffering. It was late afternoon, a Friday. A sliver of the moon hung over the jungle, anticipating the night. Kaboo heard the sound of digging. He lifted his head as best he could from where he hung over the cross of wood. His captors were digging a deep hole.

When the men finished, they leaned over Kaboo.

THEY DRAPED THE BOY OVER THE CROSSED WOOD

SAMUEL MORRIS

"Unless your father comes back with your ransom, we will bury you alive!" They pointed to the hole. "Say hello to your grave, Kru boy." They walked away to summon the chief.

The chief surveyed the hole and declared it sufficient. He signalled for another slave to be brought out to witness another beating of the pawn. A young Kru boy was led out to the clearing to watch the terrible display.

Kaboo stared blankly into space, his body crying out for relief from the unending agony of pain. Thoughts of his father and sister swirled vaguely in his mind. Nothing mattered any more.

Suddenly, a bright light broke out over Kaboo and his wooden cross. He felt a strong arm take hold of his own arm. A clear voice called to him. "Kaboo! Run! Run!"

A BRIGHT LIGHT BROKE OVER KABOO AND HIS CROSS

KABOO FELT NEW STRENGTH SURGE THROUGH HIS BODY

"Aiiee!" yelped the terrified Grebo chief and his men. The flash of light blinded their eyes. They were stunned, helpless. The young Kru slave brought out to witness the torture of his prince watched the fantastic scene with amazement.

Instantly, the ropes that bound Kaboo fell from his hands. Kaboo felt new strength surge through his body. He jumped up and ran, propelled by the voice that had urged him to flee. While the Grebos stumbled helplessly around the camp, Kaboo disappeared into the jungle.

He ran like the wind. The prince fled surefooted, guided by the light. Night fell quickly, blanketing the jungle completely with darkness. As he ran, the boy marveled at what had happened. What was this strange light? Whose voice and helping hand had reached out and set him free? The answers to his

questions would have to wait. For the moment, h
must put as much distance between him and hi
enemies as was possible.

Not knowing where he was going, Kaboo trav
eled on. He slowed his run only when he felt confi
dent that his enemies could not catch up to him fo
the moment. A dead teak tree loomed in the shad
ows. Kaboo searched it with his hands and discov
ered the trunk was hollow. He slipped inside th
tree. He could sleep safely there.

The black of night was softening into the gray o
dawn. Kaboo stayed in the tree. It would be too risk
to travel during the day. He feared being seen b
anyone. An escaped pawn was a prize to be capture
and returned to its owner.

There were other fears to wrestle with as well
The low growl of a leopard rumbled faintly i
Kaboo's ears. His heart fluttered in his chest. H
held his breath. The sound faded into the distance

KABOO TRAVELED ON

SAMUEL MORRIS

The fugitive boy relaxed. Leopards, snakes, an
wild boars were among the many dangers Kabo
would have to face in the jungle.

The young boy fell into a restless sleep. His mir
swirled with thoughts of the amazing thing that ha
happened. His father's face and his sister's soft ey
filtered through his dreams, tugging at his heart. I
knew he could not go back to his own camp.
would mean certain punishment for his peopl
Exhaustion finally triumphed over troubling thought
and the boy fell into a deep sleep.

Kaboo awoke at nightfall. He pulled himself o
of the hollow tree and stretched his body. Countle
insects and tree frogs wove a cloth of endless mus
for the night to wear. He rubbed his eyes. To h
utter amazement the light that had burst upon him
the Grebo camp was still with him! With the help
that light, Kaboo journeyed on through the jungl
He was able to find fruit, nuts, and roots to eat.

THE LIGHT WAS STILL WITH HIM!

SAMUEL MORRIS

The days passed in a blur as the prince made his way through the forest. He crossed streams, forded rivers. Lush ferns grazed his arms and legs, vines reached out with grasping arms as if to take him captive. Mangrove swamps boiled over with mud that reached up to Kaboo's knees. Driver ants crossed the jungle path, a two-inch band of fluid movement, dangerous if disturbed by a bare foot or hand.

As the distance between him and his enemies widened, the boy dared to travel during the day. Lush tree tops meshed to form a green ceiling over the forest. The sun filtered through the emerald green, sprinkling precious splatterings of light. Kaboo lost track of time. He wondered numbly where the light was leading him. Would he ever come to the end of his wanderings?

Early one morning, after what seemed like endless days, Kaboo heard a rooster crow. That could only mean one thing: civilization! He hurried forward

WOULD HE EVER COME TO THE END OF HIS WANDERINGS?

then hesitated. Who were these people? Would the
know he was an escaped pawn? Would they sen
him back to the place of horror he had left behind
Kaboo shook his head. Whoever or whatever had se
him free had surely brought him this far. He ha
nothing to lose.

Thirsty for the sight of another human being
Kaboo crept toward the noises. A soft breeze car
ried a sound to the boy's ears, a sound he felt he ha
not heard for a lifetime. Music! Someone was sin
ing! Crouching down, the young prince pulled asid
the ferns that obscured his sight.

Before his eyes stretched a field of coffee plant
The white flowers and red berries of the plan
painted the scene with bright color. Kaboo set h
sights on the one who was singing. Relief swe
through the tired traveler. It was a native Kru bo
like himself. Kaboo emerged shyly from the bus
and approached the boy.

MUSIC! SOMEONE WAS SINGING!

SAMUEL MORRIS

"Hello," he said in a small voice.

The boy looked up from his work, startled. "Hello," he greeted the stranger. He studied Kaboo's appearance. "You have come far. From the interior?"

Kaboo nodded. "Where am I now?"

"Why, you are at the coast. This is a settlemen near Monrovia."

"What day is it?"

"Today is Friday." The Kru boy smiled at Kaboo to put him at ease. "You are alone?"

Kaboo nodded. "Yes." He did not feel he coul talk about the Presence that had guided him. He di not understand it himself. "I am alone." His hea ached at the thought of his father. "I am here alone."

"Come with me," said the boy cheerfully. "M boss is a good man. He will give you a job here on th plantation. Food and clothes." He caught the fear i Kaboo's eyes. "You are safe now, brother."

Kaboo followed the boy to the main building. H

"I AM ALONE... I AM HERE ALONE"

was readily accepted and given a place to sleep in the bunkhouse. Kaboo gladly pulled on his new clothes and set out to learn the ways of the coffee plantation. He felt the cycle of terror that had ruled his life had finally come to an end.

As he adjusted to his new life, Kaboo continued to wrestle with what had transpired. He marveled at the abrupt change. One day he was hanging over a cross of wood, dying. Now he was strong and busy at work, secure and safe.

Over and over he thought about the voice and the light that had saved his life and brought him to the settlement. Who was it? It must have been some kind of spirit. Kaboo had been taught about spirits since he was a young child, but most of those spirits were to be feared and appeased with sacrifices. This spirit was different. Kaboo was hungry for answers.

Kaboo noticed there was something different about his new friend at the plantation. One day Kaboo

THIS SPIRIT WAS DIFFERENT

came into the bunkhouse and found his fellow Kru kneeling on the floor. His face and hands were turned upward. He was talking to someone.

"What are you doing?" asked the curious Kaboo.

"I am praying," replied the boy readily.

"Who are you praying to?"

"Why, I'm praying to God."

"Who is your God?" Kaboo asked, his heart pounding.

The boy looked into the young prince's eyes. "He is my Father."

Kaboo nodded. He thought it over. "Then you are talking to your Father," he decided.

The praying boy invited Kaboo to church. "Come with me to the mission this Sunday," he urged the prince. "You will hear more about God."

Kaboo attended church with his friend. He understood little of what was said, but the sense of God's presence convicted his heart. His friend explained

"I AM PRAYING"

the Gospel to him. Kaboo followed the lead of his friend and began to "talk to his Father." He prayed earnestly for answers to the aching questions in his heart. *Could a poor boy like me know God? Was it God who saved me from destruction?*

Finally, a woman came to the mission to present a lesson that would catapult Kaboo on to the path of understanding. Her name was Miss Knolls, and she came to Liberia from a college in Indiana called Taylor University. Neither Kaboo nor Miss Knolls had any idea what impact their meeting would have on Taylor University and the rest of the world.

A WOMAN CAME TO THE MISSION...

"IT IS A STORY ABOUT A MAN NAMED SAUL"

CHAPTER 5

"The story I am going to tell you is found in the Bible in the book of Acts," began the woman missionary. The interpreter faithfully translated to the audience whatever the missionary spoke. "It is a story about a man named Saul. He was filled with hatred for Jesus and his followers. He wanted all the believers in Jesus to be captured and put in prison."

Kaboo listened intently.

"One day this man was on the road traveling to a certain town in order to arrest all the followers of Christ. He was going to drag them away from their homes and imprison them."

Kaboo flinched. He knew what it was like to be taken from his home and held captive. He sat forward in his seat.

"While Saul traveled on the road, a strange thing happened. A bright light from heaven burst upon him. He fell to the ground, blind. Then he heard a voice speaking."

Miss Knolls paused, her eyes sparkling. "It was Jesus! Saul's life was changed forever! He became a Christian! Saul became a champion of the very Gospel he had tried to destroy. The light of the Gospel had come to him and saved him from a hate-filled and destructive way of life."

As the interpreter relayed to the listeners what Miss Knolls said about Saul, Kaboo's face lit up. He leapt up from his seat.

"That light! That voice! It happened to me!" he cried. "When they were whipping me and I was about to die, I heard that voice. I saw that light!" His face glowed with the revelation. "Now I know who it was who saved my life. It was Jesus!"

The gathering of people stared at the boy, astonished. Miss Knolls signalled to the interpreter to close the meeting. She headed for the young boy and

"THAT LIGHT! THAT VOICE! IT HAPPENED TO ME!"

with the help of the interpreter Kaboo told her his story. His testimony took her breath away.

"So now I know whose voice it was that told me to run," beamed the boy. "It was the voice of Jesus. What he did for that man Saul, he did for me."

Miss Knolls nodded. "Would you like to know more about Jesus?" she asked.

"Oh yes," Kaboo replied eagerly. "Tell me everything."

Miss Knolls let out a joyful laugh. "You are a missionary's dream come true!" she said.

Miss Knolls took Kaboo aside and sat him down on a bench. She explained to Kaboo the story of Jesus' life and his mission on earth. Kaboo could readily understand the concept of Jesus being taken as a pawn to save the lives of sinners. Tears streamed down his ebony face as she told how the Father gave up his Son as a pawn, and how the blood of Jesus was the payment made to redeem the people of the

SHE EXPLAINED TO KABOO THE STORY OF JESUS' LIFE

world. Sons and daughters are reconciled with their Father in heaven because the price was paid.

"I believe in this Jesus," said Kaboo softly. "His Father is my Father now."

Miss Knolls looked with joy at the African lad. God had done a mighty work. He brought the boy out of darkness into the light. She was thrilled that she could play a small part in Kaboo's story. She took him under her wing, teaching him some English. He hungrily listened to the Bible stories and lessons she taught him. Kaboo was thirsty to know more about God.

Prayer became the focus of the young prince's life. He "talked to his Father" constantly. Despite his understanding of the Gospel, a restlessness stirred in Kaboo's heart. He felt deeply the need to serve God, to tell his people about Jesus. But he felt inadequate and unworthy. Years of abuse and suffering had shattered his sense of worth. A childhood spent in

PRAYER BECAME THE FOCUS OF THE YOUNG PRINCE'S LIFE

fear and bondage had broken his spirit. How could such a one as he serve the living God?

Day and night he struggled in prayer. He agonized in prayer, crying out to God. His earnest cries were getting on his bunk mates' nerves. They told him if he was going to pray at night, he would have to pray in the jungle.

Kaboo's new house of prayer became the forest. Among the trees and vines, he lifted up his heart to his Father. Monkeys chattered back to him. Brilliantly colored birds threaded swiftly through the trees in flashes of blues, reds, and yellows. At night, the moon laced the trees in silver. Kaboo cried out to his Father. He needed Him so! He needed to give himself completely over to the Lord. The boy was desperate for God.

One night he prayed earnestly until midnight. He returned to the bunkhouse, exhausted. He flopped down on his bunk. Worn out, he lay quietly. Though

WORN OUT, HE LAY QUIETLY

his lips were silent, his heart kept right on praying
Suddenly, the room began to brim with light. Kaboc
turned over, thinking for a moment that the sun was
rising. But his bunk mates continued to sleep deeply.
They did not stir as they usually did when the sun
rose. No rooster was crowing. It was not the morning sun.

Kaboo sat up. The room was now flooded with
glorious light. At the moment the room was filled
with glory, the heavy weight on his heart was taken
away. The burden was replaced with an outpouring
of joy. He felt as light as a feather.

"Praise God!" he shouted, jumping up from his
bunk. "Praise God!" He continued to shout and leap
for joy. "I am His son! He is my Father!"

His roommates woke up to the glorious commotion. They stared at the Kru boy from the interior.

"What's going on?" someone mumbled sleepily.

"It's Kaboo," came a reply. "I think he's gone
crazy!"

THE ROOM WAS FLOODED WITH GLORIOUS LIGHT

SAMUEL MORRIS

Another man sat up, wide-eyed. "It must be a demon has got him," he said fearfully.

Kaboo could only laugh and shout for joy. His burden was gone. He knew he was in the arms of a Father who would never disappear in the jungle or be unable to care for him. He knew the One who had touched his arm at the horrible wooden cross and set him free, now held him with everlasting arms. Kaboo had become His son.

The next day, Kaboo hurried to tell Miss Knolls what had happened. The missionary listened in amazement.

"It was my adoption, Miss Knolls," said Kaboo joyfully. "God has made me His own son."

The missionary choked back tears. *How could this boy, unschooled in the Scriptures, possibly know about the theological concept of adoption?*

Another miracle, thought Miss Knolls. *Surely the hand of God is on this boy's life.*

ANOTHER MIRACLE, THOUGHT MISS KNOLLS

She pulled out her Bible and read aloud Romans 8:15: "'For ye have not received the spirit of bondage again to fear; but ye have received the Spirit of adoption, whereby we cry, Abba, Father.'"

Kaboo vigorously nodded his head. "Yes, that's it! God came to me last night. He has adopted Kaboo!"

"HE HAS ADOPTED KABOO!"

HE ASKED TO BE BAPTIZED IN THE NAME OF THE LORD

Kaboo's experience with the Lord changed him. He was a different person, filled with joy and confidence in His Father. The Lord saved him, healed him from his painful past, and filled him with the Holy Spirit. He was hungry for the Lord. As often as he could, he spent time with the missionaries to learn more from them.

Miss Knolls taught him about water baptism. He readily agreed to be baptized in the name of the Lord. When Kaboo came out of the water, Miss Knolls stood up to speak.

"My parents were poor," she said, her voice trembling. "But it was my heart's desire to serve the Lord as a missionary. I needed training. But how could I go to school with no money?" She paused and smiled at Kaboo. "The Lord has a way of providing when we cannot provide for ourselves. A banker named Samuel Morris heard about my plight and generously paid for my education at Taylor University. I stand here today, with Kaboo, the first African boy I have seen come to Christ. And so I would like to give him the name of the one who made it possible for me to be here, Samuel Morris."

(It was customary in those days for missionaries to give new believers American names.)

"From now on, you will be called Samuel Morris," Miss Knolls beamed.

Kaboo smiled. "It is a good name," he said. "Like the Samuel in the Bible, right?"

Miss Knolls nodded and shook his hand. "Congratulations on your baptism, Samuel."

"Thank you," responded the new believer.

Sammy (as he soon was called by all who knew him) was an avid student. When he wasn't working hard in the coffee fields, he was learning Bible stories from Miss Knolls. Miss Knolls also tutored him in the English language. He spent two years at

"YOU WILL BE CALLED SAMUEL MORRIS!"

SAMUEL MORRIS

the plantation. He then moved to the capital city of Monrovia. There he took up the trade of house painter.

There were many missionaries stationed in Monrovia. Sammy was eager to learn from all of them. He worked for them, helping them out in whatever way he could. He especially loved to hear their songs of praise to God. He learned many of the hymns by heart. It was obvious to the believers who came in contact with Sammy that the presence of the Lord was with this dedicated young man. When he prayed, things happened!

Three women burdened with the desire to see the people of Monrovia come to Christ met together regularly to pray. Their prayer meetings would sometimes last through the night. One night, Sammy joined their prayer meeting. He humbled himself on the floor before the Lord. For hours he pleaded for the souls of the people.

HE TOOK UP THE TRADE OF HOUSE PAINTER

SAMUEL MORRIS

At the evangelistic meetings that followed, fifty people accepted Christ as their Savior and Lord.

One day to Sammy's surprise, he met a young Kru boy whom he recognized. He was a boy from his own tribe! The boy had been captured by the same Grebo chief and kept as a slave. He had been there when prince Kaboo had been tortured.

"Kaboo!" cried the astonished boy. "You are alive! I can't believe it!"

Sammy nodded. His mind flashed with the memory of his miraculous escape. "It is a miracle I can stand here and talk with you!"

"Tell me what happened!" said the boy excitedly. "You know I was there when they tortured you. I knew you were dying, the beatings were getting so bad. But then that one night—"

Sammy grabbed the boy's arm. "You mean you saw—"

"I saw everything!" yelped the boy, his hands

"YOU MEAN YOU SAW..."

gesturing fervently. "I remember how the strange light suddenly flashed over you. I heard someone call to you!" The boy's eyes widened at the thought of it. "And then, suddenly," he whispered, "you were gone! What happened, Kaboo? What happened to you?"

Sammy's eyes filled with tears of joy. His heart thrilled because he could indeed give the explanation to his fellow Kru.

"It was the Lord, my friend!" exclaimed Sammy. "The light you saw and the voice you heard belonged to Jesus. He saved my life!" Sammy placed his hands on the astonished boy's shoulders. "He not only saved my life, he has saved my soul. He has made me His own. God is now my Father! I will never be alone again!"

The other boy's eyes filled with longing. Such comforting words! Such wondrous hope the prince was holding out to him. Sammy searched his friend's

THE OTHER BOY'S EYES FILLED WITH LONGING

face and read the desire written there.

"He can be your Father, too," spoke Sammy softly. "Would you like to pray with me?"

The boy nodded. Together they knelt and Sammy introduced his friend to Jesus.

Sammy presented the new Christian to his missionary friends. They promptly baptized him, giving him the name Henry O'Neill. Together, Sammy and Henry shared the testimony of their salvation. Many listened with wonder as Sammy talked of his miraculous escape. Henry's eyewitness account of the miracle added to the power of their testimony.

Sammy's heart stirred with an urgent desire to go back to his own people and share the Gospel with them. He spoke of it to the Reverend C. E. Smirl. Pastor Smirl was the man who headed up the missionary work in Monrovia.

"Well, Sammy, if you want to be a preacher you must get an education," said Pastor Smirl.

KABOO INTRODUCED HIS FRIEND TO JESUS

"An education?" asked Sammy. "And where should I go to get an education?"

"To America," replied Pastor Smirl. "You must go to America. And I'm afraid it will cost you one hundred dollars."

One hundred dollars was a huge sum of money to Sammy. He didn't have that kind of money. But instead of worrying about it, he talked to his Father. Conversation with his heavenly Father calmed his heart. He knew God would make a way for him to get to America.

Sammy continued to pray and seek the Lord. When a new woman missionary arrived from America, Sammy sought her out. This particular missionary spoke freely of a subject that was unfamiliar to Sammy—the Holy Spirit. Others had diligently taught him the truths of the Gospel of Jesus Christ. No one had ever spoken of the Holy Spirit as this missionary did. Sammy was captivated. To be

"YOU MUST GO TO AMERICA"

sure, he had already experienced the infilling of the Holy Spirit, but he did not know that he could become acquainted with the Holy Spirit.

The woman shared her testimony with her eager student. "When I was ready to go overseas to serve the Lord as a missionary, I was excited and frightened at the same time. I was a young girl from the far west of the United States. I traveled to New York to be sent out by Bishop Taylor. I was met by Bishop Taylor's secretary. He could see that I was feeling a bit overwhelmed."

The woman's voice softened at the memory. "The secretary began to speak to me about the Holy Spirit. He told me if I would humble myself before the Lord and wholly commit myself to Him, I would be filled with the Holy Spirit. The Holy Spirit would empower me to be a vital witness of the Gospel in Africa. His words stirred a yearning in my heart. We prayed together, and I was filled to overflowing with

SAMMY WAS CAPTIVATED

the Holy Spirit of God. When it came time to board the ship that would bear me to Africa, I was ready to go! The Comforter was with me in a way I had never experienced before."

She laughed. "My companions thought I would not do well in Africa! They would watch me as I sat alone on the boat. As I communed with the Lord in prayer, I would sometimes laugh, sometimes cry, at times just talk quietly with Him. My friends thought I was heartbroken over leaving behind a lost lover!" The woman laughed again. "Little did they know, I had come aboard with my greatest love—the Lord!"

Sammy's heart leapt for joy at her words. His talks with His Father were as sweet and intimate as the testimony shared by this new-found missionary friend.

"Please teach me more about the Holy Spirit," implored Sammy. "I want to know more about Him."

" PLEASE TEACH ME MORE ABOUT THE HOLY SPIRIT "

The woman began to open the Scriptures to the young African. She highlighted the truths in the Word concerning the Holy Spirit.

"The Scriptures teach us that the Holy Spirit is not a ghostly force. He is a counselor, a comforter. We can know Him, and we are instructed to be led by Him, to keep in step with Him."

She smiled at her eager student. "Listen to what it says in the fourteenth chapter of John's gospel: 'If you love me, keep my commandments. And I will pray the Father, and He shall give you another Comforter, that He may stay with you forever. Even the Spirit of truth, whom the world cannot receive, because it sees Him not, neither knows Him. But you know Him, for He dwells with you and shall be in you. I will not leave you orphans, I will come to you.'"

Sammy's eyes filled with tears of joy. "It is so true!" he cried. "I surely felt like an orphan bo

"LISTEN TO WHAT IT SAYS..."

before the Lord came and made me His own. Tell me more!"

In the days that followed, Sammy repeatedly visited the missionary for Bible study. She continued to explain about the work of the Holy Spirit. She explained to Sammy that it was the Holy Spirit who opens the Word to the believer, who reveals Jesus to us, who empowers us to live for Christ.

Sammy asked countless questions. He spent hours listening and learning. His hunger for God was strong. He wanted to know the Lord, wanted to walk with Him and glorify His name.

Finally, the missionary could teach her student no more.

"Sammy, I've taught you all I know. I wish I could tell you more, but I can't!" She smiled at Sammy. "I've given you all I've got. As it is, I've repeated most of it many times over!"

Sammy's face wrinkled with consternation. "We

"I'VE GIVEN YOU ALL I'VE GOT"

then," he said simply, "who taught you about the Holy Spirit?"

"A man named Stephen Merritt. He was the secretary to Bishop Taylor whom I told you about. He taught me everything I know about the Holy Spirit."

"Where is Stephen Merritt?" pressed the earnest young man.

"In New York, in America," came the reply.

Without another word, Sammy bade his teacher goodbye.

"Where are you going, Sammy?" she asked curiously.

The young man turned, his head tilted quizzically as if he marveled that she didn't know where he was going.

"Why, I'm going to America to see Stephen Merritt. He will teach me more about the Holy Ghost." He smiled and nodded farewell.

"WHY, I'M GOING TO AMERICA TO SEE STEPHEN MERRITT"

SAMUEL MORRIS

The amazed woman watched him go. Her own heart stirred at the sight of a young man whose only passion was to know the Lord—a young man who would go wherever he had to in order to learn more about Him.

THE AMAZED WOMAN WATCHED HIM GO

"MY FATHER TOLD ME YOU WOULD TAKE ME TO AMERICA"

CHAPTER 7

Sammy headed immediately for the coast. When he arrived at the beach, he caught sight of a ship anchored in the distance. The water pulsated with shimmering light. Shielding his eyes from the bright afternoon sun, Sammy talked to his Father. After praying, he knew the ship was the one that would carry him to America. He dug his bare feet into the warm sand and waited patiently for someone from the ship to come by.

Sammy watched as a small boat was lowered from the ship. The captain and several of his men rowed their way to shore. Sammy approached them.

"Excuse me, sir," Sammy addressed the captain. "My Father told me you would take me to America in your ship."

The seaman looked at the young African with contempt. "And where is your father?" he inquired gruffly.

"He is in heaven," replied Sammy.

The captain looked at his companions. He rolled his eyes. He snorted with disgust. "I don't take passengers. Especially black passengers," he spat. "Out of my way!" He strode past Sammy, shoving him aside.

Sammy watched the captain and his men walk away. He was not discouraged by the captain's refusal. He knew what his Father had said. Sammy sat down next to the small boat and waited.

At dusk the captain returned. To his chagrin, the African boy was still on the beach, standing next to the boat. The boy approached the captain again. His request was again refused.

The sun slipped below the far horizon. Reds and purples enflamed the sky with color. Sammy lay down in the sand. He spent the night praying. He was assured that the next time he talked to the captain, he

"OUT OF MY WAY!"

would receive a favorable answer. Sammy fell asleep with a smile on his face.

The following morning was a busy one for the captain and his crew. All day they hauled the cargo they had acquired to the ship. Sammy helped out in any way he could. When finally he saw the captain, he spoke to him with quiet confidence. "My Father says you will let me come with you this time," he said with a smile.

The captain was tempted to give the young man a swift kick. But two of his crew had deserted the ship the night before. Now he was short-handed. He would need this boy to work. The man rubbed the steely stubble on his chin. The boy was Kru, and they were known to be good seamen.

"All right," said the captain. "You can join my crew." He set his steely eyes on the boy. "What do you want for pay?"

"I want to go to New York to see Stephen

"ALL RIGHT... YOU CAN JOIN MY CREW"

SAMUEL MORRIS

Merritt."

The captain stared at the boy. *He's a strange one,* he thought. He signalled to his men to let the boy get in to the boat.

Sammy's face glowed with joy as the oars of the boat cut into the water, propelling them toward the ship. His Father's promise was coming to pass. Sammy was on his way to America. He was on his way to gaining his heart's desire—more knowledge about the Holy Spirit of God.

The three masts of the ship pointed upward to the azure sky. Sammy climbed aboard and waited for the captain's orders.

The captain ordered his men to weigh anchor. The ship pulled away from the harbor. Liberia disappeared into the distance.

"This is my boat," boomed the captain. "She's a tramp vessel, only three hundred and fifty feet long. It makes for a rough ride." He peered at the Kru boy

LIBERIA DISAPPEARED INTO THE DISTANCE

who stood before him. "You're an experienced boatman, I assume? You are a Kru. How long have you worked on the coast? What's your specialty?"

Sammy shook his head. "I have no experience on boats. My people did not live on the coast."

The captain's mouth spewed forth curses. "You mean you lived in the interior? You're not from the coast? You're worthless to me!" He started for the young man. "I ought to throw you overboard right now and save myself a heap of trouble." He glowered at Sammy. "You haven't been sick until you've been seasick! You won't be able to do any work!"

"Please sir, do not be angry," pleaded Sammy. "I will work for you every day until we reach New York. I will be able to work, you'll see."

"All right, then," said the captain. He looked around the ship. "You'll work the masts. Clancey!" he yelled to one of his men. "Show this idiot how to reef the sails. I want him working the masts."

"I OUGHT TO THROW YOU OVERBOARD RIGHT NOW"

SAMUEL MORRIS

"I won't disappoint you, sir," responded Sammy. "I will work hard. I must get to New York to see Stephen Merritt."

The captain walked away shaking his head. *That boy just doesn't give up,* he thought.

Sammy walked the deck to get his bearings. To his surprise he discovered a young man his own age lying on the deck. He was groaning with pain.

The African youth knelt beside the stricken sailor.

"What happened to you?" Sammy asked gently.

The boy looked up into Sammy's brown face. "I was injured in an accident," he whispered. "It's bad," he moaned. "I was the cabin boy. Now I can't even walk."

"I will talk to my Father about it," replied the concerned Sammy. He lifted his face to heaven and asked the Lord to make the suffering boy well again. To the surprise of the stricken sailor, strength and healing flowed through his body. He was instantly

"I WAS INJURED IN AN ACCIDENT"

healed!

Leaping up from the floor, the boy grabbed the newcomer by the hand.

"I am well! Your prayer worked! How can I ever thank you!"

Sammy smiled. "Don't thank me. Thank the Lord Jesus. He is the healer."

The young sailor let out a whoop. He ran about the deck, exhilarated with new health. He stopped long enough to study Sammy's face.

"You're new on the ship," he said. "You look hungry."

Sammy nodded. "I haven't eaten in three days."

"Well, come with me," said the sailor. "I'll take you to the galley."

The cook took one look at Sammy and refused to give him food. "I don't serve Negroes," he said with a sneer.

The cabin boy took Sammy to his sleeping

THE YOUNG SAILOR LET OUT A WHOOP

quarters. "I'll be right back." He returned to the galley.

"I could eat a horse," the cabin boy said to the cook. "Pile it on, Smithers."

The cook obliged the sailor. "Good to see you up and about, Johnny."

Johnny smiled and took his heaping plate. He quickly returned to Sammy and shared the food with him.

"It's the least I can do for you," he said to the grateful Sammy. "If it weren't for your prayer, I'd still be lying on that deck."

"God is good," replied Sammy. It was no surprise to Sammy that God answers prayer. Sammy knew he had a faithful, loving Father.

It was obvious the voyage was not going to be an easy one for the Kru boy. Although the crew of the ship was a wide assortment of men from all over the world, Sammy was the only African. He became the

"GOD IS GOOD"

object of scorn and ridicule. The men impatiently taught him to work the mast, cursing and cuffing him at every turn. But Sammy was filled with the Holy Spirit. His peace was boundless. He bore each indignity with patience and forgiveness. A supernatural strength and kindness flowed through him. Although Sammy did not like climbing up the mast, he worked diligently at his task.

Securing the sails was hard work; in windy conditions it was especially difficult. Three days out to sea, a tropical storm burst forth with fury. Sammy was tied to his mast so he could reef the sails without falling overboard. The darkened sky brooded over the tramp vessel with vengeance. Strong winds tore at the boat, causing it to turn on its side again and again. The winds roared, and the ocean answered with boiling foam and roiling waves. Sammy told the Lord he was not afraid of the storm. "I know You will take care of me. But, Fathe,r I do not like being

"I KNOW YOU WILL LOOK AFTER ME"

up on the mast. Please make a way for me to do a different job."

Each time the boat groaned to its side, Sammy was immersed in the sea. He gagged on the salty water, swallowing large amounts. It made him violently ill. His arms fell weakly to his sides. He was helpless.

A sailor spotted the trouble and untied Sammy. He crumpled to the floor.

The captain walked by and kicked Sammy. "I knew you'd get sick and be of no use!" He walked away without giving further thought to the stricken young man.

Sammy immediately began to speak to the One who knew him best and loved him most. While the deck pitched and heaved and water swept by Sammy, the sick young man lifted up his hands and his heart to his Father.

"Father, you know I made a promise to the cap-

"I KNEW YOU'D GET SICK AND BE OF NO USE!"

tain to work for him every day until we reach New York. I cannot work when I am so sick. Please take this sickness from me, Father."

The Lord answered His child and Sammy got up from the deck, restored to health. He was never again sick aboard the ship.

THE LORD ANSWERED HIS CHILD

"WHAT ARE YOU DOING HERE?"

CHAPTER 8

The next day Sammy headed for the mast. A voice called to him. It was the cabin boy.

"Sammy, I saw you at the mast when the storm hit," he said. "I know you don't like working the mast. Well, how about a trade?" he continued. "I don't like working below in the captain's cabin. I'd rather be up on the mast. Let's trade jobs."

Sammy gladly agreed. As he walked toward the captain's quarters, he whispered a heartfelt thanks to his Father.

The door to the cabin was ajar. As Sammy entered the room, the captain looked up from his desk in a drunken stupor. His eyes focused on the ebony figure that stood before him.

"What are you doing here?" he demanded, his voice thick with liquor.

SAMUEL MORRIS

Sammy explained the trade he had made with the cabin boy. Without a word, the cruel captain raised his fist and knocked the young man unconscious to the filthy floor.

When Sammy came to, he rose to his feet. He picked up his rags and bucket of water and began to clean the cabin. The captain watched the boy in amazement. Not only did Sammy not retaliate, but there was a look of peace on his face. The power of forgiveness touched the rough man's heart.

Sammy looked over at the captain. "Do you know about Jesus?" he asked.

At the name of Jesus, memories of his mother were triggered in the captain's mind. Faint recollections of Sunday school and Bible verses floated to the surface of his heart.

"May I pray for you?" asked Sammy.

The captain nodded. He listened as Sammy prayed the captain would discover the love of God in Jesus

"DO YOU KNOW ABOUT JESUS?"

SAMUEL MORRIS

Christ. Something began to stir in the captain's heart. He yearned for the peace and strength that the young Kru possessed. After prayer, he left Sammy to inspect the ship for damage from the storm. The captain's stubbled face was wrinkled in thought. There was something about Samuel Morris that he just couldn't understand.

The boat had been badly damaged by the storm. Repair work was in full swing for two weeks. Holes had to be caulked, breakage repaired. Pumps were utilized to keep water from capsizing the boat. Sammy was assigned to one of the many pumps.

In an attempt to keep the crew in good spirits while doing such arduous work, the captain supplied the men with rum and cane juice. The alcohol burned in the men's veins. They became loose with their tongues. Tempers flared. Sammy became the butt of cruel jibes and threats.

One man in particular hated Sammy. He was a

THERE WAS SOMETHING ABOUT SAMUEL MORRIS...

SAMUEL MORRIS

Malayan. Cruel and cold-hearted, he carried a large knife at all times. He wasn't afraid to use it on any man who came against him. The man despised Africans and often boasted that he would kill the Kru boy whenever he got the chance.

His chance came. After the boat was repaired, the captain rewarded the crew's hard work with a generous supply of rum. The drinking resulted in the usual commotion of hard laughter and hard talk. An argument broke out among the men. The Malayan took offense. He pulled out his cutlass, his eyes glittering darkly with hatred. He would cut to pieces the ones who had taunted him.

Suddenly a small dark form stood in the Malayan's path. It was Sammy.

"Don't kill, don't kill," Sammy pleaded, his hand upraised.

Shocked by the boy's boldness, the man hesitated. Quickly regaining his composure, the Malayan saw

"DON'T KILL, DON'T KILL"

his chance to kill the Kru. He lifted his cutlass above his head, murder sparking his eyes.

Sammy stood his ground. The compassion burning in his face met and overcame the hatred in the Malayan's eyes. The angry man lowered his cutlass. He turned and walked away.

The sailors watching the scene had fully expected to see blood flow on the deck. They stood dumbfounded and silent. The fury of one of the most dangerous men on board had been snuffed out by the young African.

The captain came on deck in time to see the amazing sight. He turned back to his cabin. What power did that Kru possess? How did he manage to bring peace to such a volatile moment? He beckoned Sammy to follow him.

The cabin had been transformed under Sammy's care. It looked like new, sparkling with cleanliness. "The Spirit will not live where filth remains," Sammy

THE ANGRY MAN LOWERED HIS CUTLASS

often said as he tackled each job. The captain looked around the changed room and realized he needed to be changed as well.

"I want to thank you for preventing a big brawl out there," said the captain. He cleared his throat. "Will you pray for me?" he asked Sammy.

Sammy smiled and knelt with the man who had cursed at him, kicked him, and knocked him unconscious. He helped his captain pray a prayer of repentance. Now the captain possessed a new heart! They prayed together that the rest of the crew would come to know the unsurpassing love of Christ.

With the ship repaired, they continued their travel along the coast of Africa. The influence of the Lord's presence began to change the atmosphere on the ship. The captain summoned crew members to the cabin for prayers. Sammy's constant singing of the hymns he had learned became contagious. The sailors started joining in whenever they had the

"WILL YOU PRAY FOR ME?"

chance. Rum was no longer offered as a reward. Peace began to reign.

The grace of God reached the cruel man who had pulled his cutlass on Sammy. The Malay had become seriously ill. He was dying. When Sammy found out about it, he hurried to the man's bunk. Kneeling down, Sammy talked to his Father about the man's fatal illness. The healing power of God fell on the Malayan. He was instantly healed! His gratitude to the African boy was boundless. Now he would do anything for Sammy!

The ship's hold was nearly full of cargo. The captain decided on one last stop. They loaded the boat with goods to trade. The lookout in the crow's nest was ordered to stand by. If there were any indication of trouble, he was to signal the captain.

The boat was lowered into the water. The island they were heading for looked peaceful. Suddenly the lookout spotted several light boats being thrust into

THE HEALING POWER OF GOD FELL UPON THE MALAYAN

the water from the beach. Through his spyglass he watched many natives manning the boats, armed with clubs and knives. Feverishly, the lookout waved his arms to signal the captain to return to the ship. The heavy-laden boat was difficult to maneuver. They headed back toward the ship, but the weight of the cargo slowed them down. The natives in the slender boats quickly caught up. The captain and his men fired their guns. Numerous attackers fell into the water. Gaining time for a getaway, the boat barely reached the ship before being attacked again. The captain and his men quickly boarded the ship.

"Get below!" the captain shouted to Sammy. Sammy's chest pounded with fear. Memories of the murderous attacks of the Grebos flooded his mind. He ran to the cabin. Quickly he locked up the captain's valuables and bolted the door behind him.

The fighting on deck reached a feverish pitch. The crew on board had fired on the attacking boats, but

THE NATIVES IN THE SLENDER BOAT QUICKLY CAUGHT UP

several of the attackers had managed to reach the ship. They clambered aboard and swarmed the deck like driver ants. Gunfire punctuated the air again and again. Shouts and cries of agony exploded from the throats of those who were cut down by bullets or knives.

Sammy knelt below, shivering with fear and concern for his friends fighting above on the deck. He poured out his heart in intercession for them.

Finally, a strong wind blew in and pitched the boat. The heavy rocking of the ship prevented anyone else from climbing aboard. The captain and his men fought fiercely and defeated their attackers. The roar of battle diminished and gave way to somber silence.

Sammy reemerged on deck. The sight that met his eyes was devastating. The stain of blood was everywhere. Body after body was thrown overboard. Sammy grieved as he watched those whom he had

SAMMY GRIEVED...

come to know as friends fall to their watery grav

The captain was badly wounded. Sammy hurrie
to his side and helped him down to his cabin. Th
captain passed out on his bunk from loss of bloo
Sammy quickly cleansed the wounds and boun
them.

When the captain came to, Sammy was at his sid
He put his arm around Sammy's young black shou
ders. "You were praying, weren't you, Sammy?" th
captain said weakly.

Sammy nodded.

"Well, my friend, the Lord answered your prayer
We were outnumbered ten to one. We should hav
lost! The Lord answered your prayers. We are saf
now."

Sammy urged the captain to rest. Then he wer
above to see who else was wounded and neede
care. For the rest of the voyage, Sammy tended
the sailors. His gentle hands dressed their wound

"WELL, MY FRIEND, THE LORD ANSWERED YOUR PRAYERS"

SAMUEL MORRIS

His caring heart and joyful voice lightened the spirit of the entire crew. The Light of the World shone through Samuel Morris, lighting the dark and lonely corners of many of the sailors' hearts.

THE LIGHT OF THE WORLD SHONE THROUGH SAMUEL MORRIS

"THERE IT IS, SAMMY... NEW YORK!"

CHAPTER 9

"There it is, Sammy," pointed one of the sailors. "New York!"

Sammy's face lit up with excitement. New York! At long last, after almost six months at sea, he had reached his destination. The buildings of the city rose above the harbor like a bustling crowd. Sammy had never before seen so many buildings at one place.

"Look!" said the sailor. "That's the Lady of Liberty!"

The Statue of Liberty raised her torch high above the gleaming water of the harbor. Sammy was amazed at the huge statue. But his heart yearned for only one thing. To find Stephen Merritt. He remembered the words of the woman missionary: "Stephen Merritt taught me everything I know about the Holy Spirit.

He's in New York, in America."

The late afternoon sun cast a golden hue over the city. The water rushed smoothly toward the dock lapping its sides and breaking away again with swaying rhythm.

"Well, we made it!" boomed the captain's voice. "And what a lovely Friday it is, too!" He smiled at Sammy. "You certainly earned your pay."

Tears fell from Sammy's eyes. It had been a Friday when the voice had urged him to run from the Grebos. It had been a Friday when he had reached the settlement near Monrovia. And now he had arrived at his destination on the same day.

"My emancipation day!" he cried joyfully. He turned his face toward heaven. "I thank You for this day, Father. I will ever dedicate Fridays to you. I will neither eat nor drink on this day, but will hunger and thirst after You." With that began Sammy's pattern of fasting on Friday every week. This act of worship

"WELL, WE MADE IT!"

surely touched the heart of the One who gave up His life on a Friday centuries before.

The crew rallied around Sammy and gave him a suit of clothes and a pair of shoes. Captain and crew alike tearfully bade goodbye to the boy who had showed them the way of love. The boundaries of each race had melted before the power of God's love. They would never forget Samuel Morris. Samuel Morris hoped they would never forget the One who had kept them all in His care.

Sammy ventured down the gangplank to the wharf. There was one goal in his mind. Find Stephen Merritt. He called to the first person he saw walking past the wharf.

"Excuse me, sir," said Sammy. "Can you tell me where I can find Stephen Merritt?"

Out of the hundreds of people who could have been walking by, this person was a homeless man who had often found help and food at Stephen

THERE WAS ONE GOAL IN HIS MIND

Merritt's mission.

"Well, this is Pike Street," responded the man. "Mr. Merritt's way over on Eighth Avenue. That's three or four miles from here." He studied the young man from Africa. "I'll take you to him for a dollar," he said, scenting a profit.

"All right," said Sammy. Sammy did not have a dollar. He didn't have any money. But he knew his Father would provide. Hadn't the Reverend C. E. Smirl told him he'd need one hundred dollars to get to America? And here he was, in America. The Lord had provided passage to the United States. He would provide the one dollar this man was demanding.

The man led Sammy up and down the streets of New York. They reached Eighth Avenue and arrived at their destination just as Stephen Merritt was slipping his key into the lock of his office door.

"That's him!" Sammy's guide pointed to the man at the door.

"I'LL TAKE YOU TO HIM FOR A DOLLAR"

SAMUEL MORRIS

Sammy hurried up to the stranger. "Stephen Merritt?"

"Yes," replied Mr. Merritt.

"I am Samuel Morris," said Sammy. "I have just come from Africa to talk to you about the Holy Spirit."

Merritt regarded the young black man with surprise. "Do you have any letters of introduction from your church leaders?" he inquired.

"No. I did not have time to wait," responded Sammy.

Stephen Merritt smiled at the eagerness that faced him. "I have to go over to Jane Street just now for prayer meeting. You go into our mission next door here and wait for me. Make yourself at home. When I return, we'll see what we can do for you."

Sammy nodded in agreement. "All right, Stephen Merritt."

"Hey, what about my dollar!" interjected Sammy's guide.

"I AM SAMUEL MORRIS"

"Oh, Stephen Merritt pays all my bills now," responded Sammy with confidence.

Mr. Merritt smiled at his new student. "Certainly," he said, handing the man a dollar.

Sammy nodded his thanks. Mr. Merritt directed him through the door of the mission and then hurried off to prayer meeting. When he returned hours later, he had the surprise of his life.

The young black man was kneeling on the platform of the mission. Seventeen men were on their faces on the floor surrounding Sammy. They were weeping and praying in repentance. Sammy had shared his testimony of God's grace and salvation. The power of God had fallen on the men, and they were cryng out to God. The scene played out the truth found in John 6:44: "No one can come to me [says Jesus] unless the Father who sent me draws him."

Merritt was stunned. This young man, who

MERRITT WAS STUNNED

SAMUEL MORRIS

virtually had no education or training and who came from what was then considered a "heathen" continent, had led nearly twenty people to Christ on his first night in America! Stephen Merritt recognized immediately that Samuel Morris had been empowered and sent to the United States by the Lord.

"You're coming home with me," declared Mr. Merritt. He brought Sammy out to the coach and invited him to climb aboard. Sammy was fascinated by the beautiful team of horses that pulled the carriage. He couldn't take his eyes off them!

They arrived in style at Mr. Merritt's home. Mrs. Merritt greeted her husband at the door.

"Why, who is this?" she asked her husband when she saw the young African standing at her door.

"This is an angel in ebony, Dolly, my dear," replied Mr. Merritt. "Meet Samuel Morris, from Liberia."

"What are you going to do with him?" stammered

"MEET SAMUEL MORRIS, FROM LIBERIA"

SAMUEL MORRIS

an astounded Dolly Merritt.

"I'm going to give him the Bishop's room," replied Mr. Merritt.

He led Sammy to the guest room that Bishop William Taylor used whenever he was in New York. William Taylor was a bishop in the Methodist Episcopal Church. Stephen drew out one of the bishop's long dressing gowns. Sammy had never worn pajamas before or slept in a bed. Mr. Merritt explained to him what to do.

When he came back to check on Sammy, he laughed out loud. Sammy's skinny frame was swallowed up in the large white night shirt. Sammy grinned at his new friend. He reached out his hand. "Let's pray," suggested Sammy.

They knelt beside the bed. Sammy thanked his Father for bringing him safely to New York. His heart rejoiced at the hand of God in his life. There was so much to be thankful for!

SAMMY GRINNED AT HIS NEW FRIEND

SAMUEL MORRIS

The presence of God filled the room as Samuel prayed. Mr. Merritt bowed his head in awe. More than ever he knew this young man was wholly dedicated to God and sent to America for a purpose.

The next morning, Sammy was not in his room. The Merritts discovered him in the stables, helping the groom with the horses. Calling to Sammy, Mr. and Mrs. Merritt had him sit at the table with their family. It was the first time the family had ever eaten a meal with someone from Africa. Mr. Merritt dispelled the tension of his family with his easy manner. The food set before them was different from what Sammy ate in his homeland. Mr. Merritt taught him about the types of food in America and the customs of eating. Sammy was a willing and hungry student!

On Sunday, Mr. Merritt invited Sammy to attend Sunday school with him. "I am the superintendent of the school. I would like you to speak to the students."

THE MERRITTS DISCOVERED HIM IN THE STABLES

SAMUEL MORRIS

Sammy smiled. "I have never been to a Sunday school before. I would be happy to go."

They arrived at the church. Mr. Merritt introduced the visitor.

"This is Samuel Morris," he explained with a smile. "He has come from Africa to talk to your superintendent about the Holy Spirit. I have asked him to speak to you this morning about the things of the Lord."

Mr. Merritt left Sammy to tend to something elsewhere in the church. When he returned, there was Sammy on the platform. The altar was crowded with young people. They were kneeling and weeping in prayer. The room was electric with the power of God.

"It was his prayer," said one student. "When he began to pray, it turned me inside out. Jesus is working through him!"

Stephen Merritt made up his mind to make a way

THERE WAS SAMMY ON THE PLATFORM

for Sammy to go to college. At Taylor University Sammy could further his studies in the Bible. He could be equipped to carry on the ministry God had so obviously called him to. Mr. Merritt shared his plan with the Sunday school.

Later a group of the young people approached their superintendent.

"We want to help Sammy go to college. We've formed the Samuel Morris Missionary Society. The idea is to raise up all he needs for school—money, clothes, and books."

Mr. Merritt wholeheartedly supported their efforts. In the days ahead, the young people were able to gather together everything Sammy would need to go to Taylor University.

One Saturday morning, Mr. Merritt was to conduct a funeral service for a prominent citizen in Harlem, New York. He brought Sammy along with him in the coach. "I'll show you some of the sights

"WE WANT TO HELP SAMMY GO TO COLLEGE"

of the city," said Mr. Merritt.

To the clip-clopping of the elegant horses, Mr. Merritt pointed out Central Park. "And there's the Grand Opera House," he pointed to the majestic building.

"Stephen Merritt," interrupted Sammy. "Do you never pray in a coach?"

"Why, yes, I often pray while I'm riding along," said Mr. Merritt.

Sammy placed his large black hand over Stephen's white one. "We will pray."

He led Mr. Merritt to kneel. Merritt looked in amazement at the young man and wondered what would happen next. He had prayed before in a coach, but never on his knees! The prayer that came forth from Samuel Morris changed Stephen Merritt's life.

"Holy Spirit," said Sammy softly, urgently. "I have come all the way from Africa to talk to Stephen Merritt about You. Stephen Merritt talks about the

THE PRAYER WOULD CHANGE STEPHEN MERRITT'S LIFE

city and the sights to see. I want so much to learn more of You, to hear more about You. Take out of his heart the things of the earth, and so fill him with Yourself that he cannot speak or write or talk of anything but You."

The fire of the Comforter fell on Stephen Merritt and burned in his heart. Here was a man who had taught others about the Holy Spirit and had been prayed for by mighty men of God. But the child-like prayer of this supposedly "uneducated" young man from another country pulled back the veil and showed Stephen Merritt how little he did know. Sammy had come to be taught by Merritt. Instead it was Merritt who was taught by the young African.

Arriving at the funeral, Merritt preached a word of comfort and salvation that so moved the listeners that three men came forward and knelt at the casket to receive Christ. Sammy sat among the attendants, glowing with the joy of being in such a blessed place,

THE FIRE OF THE COMFORTER FELL ON STEPHEN MERRITT

where life was so gently commemorated at death and where Jesus was glorified.

At the Merritt home, Sammy was asked to say grace. His prayer moved Dolly to tears. The prejudice and reserve in her heart was wiped away. "Our home is yours, Sammy. Stay with us as long as you like."

Stephen Merritt explained to Sammy that he felt he could help him most by sending him to Taylor University in Indiana. It was staffed by godly people who could help Sammy grow in his knowledge of the Scriptures. Sammy agreed to the plan. He wanted so much to return to his own land and teach his people about the Lord.

A letter was written to C. B. Stemen, medical doctor, preacher, and former president of Taylor University. He immediately showed the letter to Dr. Thaddeus Reade, president of Taylor.

"Merritt says he's a diamond in the rough,"

SAMMY AGREED TO THE PLAN

explained Reverend Stemen. "Probably eighteen years old. He says his church at Jane Street will clothe him and pay for his passage to Indiana."

"And would we be willing to take him in and pay for his education," echoed Dr. Reade, reading from the letter.

He put the letter on his desk and faced his colleague. "I have longed to help students with no money get a college education." He rubbed his chin. "The university is young and struggling with debt. Can we take on the financial responsibility of this lad from Africa?"

The men prayed together. Both concluded it was the Lord's will to accept the new student. A letter was sent right away. "Send him on," it read. "God will take care of him."

"SEND HIM ON", IT READ, "GOD WILL TAKE CARE OF HIM"

RIDING IN A TRAIN WAS ANOTHER NEW EXPERIENCE

CHAPTER 10

The steam engine train steamed across the country, bearing the awestruck Sammy Morris. Riding in a train was another new experience for the young man. The train pulled into Fort Wayne, Indiana, on a cold December Friday. Someone met him at the station and brought him to the university.

Sammy was ushered into the office of the president of Taylor University.

"Welcome to Taylor, Samuel," Dr. Reade greeted the young man warmly. "Our first job is to assign you a room!"

"I will take the room that no one else wants. That is fine for me," responded Sammy.

Dr. Reade turned away from the boy to hide the tears that sprang to his eyes. The humility and sincerity of this new student pierced the heart of the college president. Over the years, he had allotted rooms to countless students. Not one had ever offered to take a room no one else would take! *I wonder, would I do the same?* thought Dr. Reade.

Sammy was given a room and a tour of the campus. At chapel service, a call was made for volunteers to tutor the new student. Before he could take regular college classes, Sammy needed to be tutored in the basics of a high school education. Several people volunteered. They subsequently found that working with Samuel Morris proved to be a real blessing. He worked hard. He was especially good at studying Scripture.

While Sammy and the other students pursued their studies, Dr. Reade worked hard to keep the university financially afloat. Times were hard for the college. Dr. Reade visited a small Methodist Church in a small town in northern Indiana and shared the need for support. He spoke of their newest student, the young man from Africa. He appealed to the

HE WORKED HARD

SAMUEL MORRIS

people to give financial aid to support Samuel Morris' education.

After the service, someone handed Reade fifty cents. It was discouraging. But on his way to catch his train, a man called to him from inside a butcher shop. It was Josiah Kichler. He handed Dr. Reade a five dollar bill.

"I feel led by the Spirit to contribute this to your faith fund," said the butcher.

Dr. Reade thanked him and boarded his train. Instead of discouragement, his heart rang with hope. Faith fund. The words resounded in the college president's ears. "We shall have a Samuel Morris Faith Fund," decided Dr. Reade. "All contributions shall be used to help Sammy get the education he needs."

The fund proved to be part of God's plan. Contributions started to come in on a regular basis. Sammy insisted that Mr. Reade use it to pay only for his

"WE SHALL HAVE A SAMUEL MORRIS FAITH FUND"

necessities. He wanted none of the money for himself. The fund grew and was utilized to help other needy students gain an education.

Samuel Morris ignited the campus and the community as soon as he arrived. He inquired about a black congregation and was directed to the African Methodist Episcopal Church located on East Wayne Street. He arrived in time to hear the sermon, but instead of taking a seat, Sammy walked up to the minister and asked permission to speak.

The minister looked with surprise at the new visitor. There was something about the young man that prompted the minister to give in to his request.

Sammy took the pulpit and began to pray. Once again, the hand of God was moved by the child-like and heartfelt prayers of the earnest believer. The presence of God fell on the people. They began to cry out in prayer, some weeping in awe and repentance, others laughing with the joy of the Lord.

THE MINISTER LOOKED WITH SURPRISE AT THE VISITOR

SAMUEL MORRIS

Revival had come to the church on East Wayne Street. The service lingered on. The people basked in the presence of the Lord.

Local newspapers heard of the event and printed editorials. Almost overnight, Samuel Morris became a household name in the city of Fort Wayne!

On campus, Sammy's walk with God excited his fellow students. His joy in learning, his simple faith, his powerful prayers—these all turned the eyes of students and staff alike to examine their own walks with God. In the hands of God, Samuel Morris became a missionary to the students and faculty of Taylor University.

The university was struggling with financial difficulties. The time came when it was thought the doors to the college would have to be closed. The university needed to move from its campus; there was no place to go. But with the help of the growing Faith Fund, and the inspiration of Sammy himself,

LOCAL NEWSPAPERS HEARD OF THE EVENT

the board pulled together. A former student named Lindley Baldwin encouraged the board to move the college to Upland, Indiana. The property and monies needed for the move were supplied. Essentially, God used Sammy to save the college from closing!

One day Sammy entered Dr. Reade's office with a surprising request.

"Is it all right if I stop studying for awhile and go to work?" he asked.

"Why, Sammy?"

"I need to make enough money to bring Henry O'Neill over to America. He would be a much better student than I am."

"Now, Sammy, you go talk to your Father about this. See what He has to say about your friend."

Sammy quickly agreed and disappeared to his room. When he returned to Dr. Reade, it was obvious the answer given was a good one. Sammy's face glowed with happiness.

"I NEED TO BRING HENRY O'NEILL OVER TO AMERICA"

SAMUEL MORRIS

"Well?" inquired Dr. Reade.

"My Father says Henry will be coming over soon. He is taking care of everything."

Dr. Reade wrote to the proper authorities and discovered that one of the missionaries who worked with Henry was indeed bringing him over to be educated!

The students at Taylor came to know and love the young man from Africa. In the hall that passed Sammy's room, he could often be heard "talking to his Father." Late at night, early in the morning, Sammy's passion was to pray. When he prayed, he gave his full attention to the Lord. If someone knocked at his door while he was in prayer, the knock would not be acknowledged until Sammy was finished talking with his Father.

Once Dr. Reade passed by Sammy's room. He quietly opened the door. There knelt Sammy, his face lifted toward heaven, much like the boy who

"MY FATHER SAYS HENRY WILL BE COMING OVER SOON"

knelt in the bunkhouse in Liberia, the boy throu
whom Sammy discovered prayer.

The influence of Sammy's prayers leaked from
room into the halls of the college. Students we
drawn to him. Anyone who entered his room w
asked to read the Bible aloud. Sammy's fame spre.
Visitors came from various places to meet with
young man from Africa.

One day a confirmed atheist visited Sammy in
room. He was prepared to argue against the exi
ence of God. Sammy asked him to read a passage
the Bible aloud to him. The man refused.

"I don't believe in that book," scoffed the athe
"It's nothing but a bunch of fairy tales!"

Sammy drew in his breath, amazed and filled w
compassion for the man. "What! Your Father spea
and you don't believe? Your Brother speaks, a
you don't believe? The Sun shines, and you do
believe it? God is your Father, Christ is your broth

"I DON'T BELIEVE IN THAT BOOK!"

SAMUEL MORRIS

the Holy Spirit is your Sun. Let me pray for you.
The man became a Christian.

"LET ME PRAY FOR YOU"

SAMMY LOVED THE OUTDOORS

CHAPTER 11

Sammy became very involved with the churches in the area. He was an active member of the Berry Street Methodist Episcopal Church, and continued to attend services at the Methodist Episcopal Church on East Wayne Street.

When evangelistic services were held at the old skating rink in town, Sammy was there. When the hymns were sung, Sammy's voice rang out with singular joy. He was always on the platform, ready to pray with anyone in need.

All racial and economic barriers fell wherever Sammy was; he prayed for white, black, rich, or poor. The results were always the same. People were touched by God.

Sammy loved the outdoors and often took walks to drink in the beauty of the land. The singing of the birds and fragrance of the flowers filled Sammy with joy. The first time he saw snow fall, he rushed out to examine the mysterious mantle of beauty. He viewed it as an awesome message from God.

"God must be saying something to us," he exclaimed to Dr. Reade. "Only God could create something as beautiful as this!" He scooped some of the white wonder into his hand to get a closer look. Soon it was gone.

"Where did it go, Dr. Reade?" asked an astonished Sammy. "It left this water in my hand!" He shook his head in wonder. "The Lord is sure good to you folks in Indiana!"

Sammy's body was not used to the cold climate. That winter his ears were affected by the freezing temperatures. He was in great pain. As was his custom, he talked to his Father about it. The pain left him, and he went about his busy schedule.

Sammy's days were filled with study, worship, and fellowship. A young man from Armenia arrived

"GOD MUST BE SAYING SOMETHING TO US"

at the college, thanks to the Faith Fund. He studied along with Sammy, learning English, basic skills, and Bible with the help of tutors. His goal was to return to his homeland and help his mother preach the Gospel there.

The young man from Africa talked often of his dream, too. His heart burned with the desire to return to Liberia and share the Gospel with his people.

He would often take walks with his friends. Together they would talk of their plans for their lives. Sammy would talk of Liberia.

"When I go back," he would say, "I will gather the children together. We will sit in a circle on the sand. I will tell them all about Jesus." His face warmed at the thought. "I know they will go into the forest to pray. Then they will have joy."

Sammy had a heart for the children of his people. He remembered the hardships of his own childhood

"I WILL TELL THEM ALL ABOUT JESUS"

and the uncertainty of his life then. He was ever filled with joy that God had ransomed the young prince Kaboo. He wanted other children to know the same glorious love.

The winter of 1892 hit Indiana with ferocity. Below zero temperatures took their toll on Sammy's body. He came down with a bad cold. But nothing would stop the young man from attending all the church meetings during the week. He was always there to sing and pray, to bask in the presence of his Lord.

His cold worsened, but Sammy continued his studies. His weakened body finally succumbed to serious illness. Dr. Stemen had him immediately admitted to St. Joseph's Hospital.

His friends came often to visit him.

"I do not understand this," he would say with a puzzled look. "Last winter, when my ears were hurting me, I asked my Father and He healed me.

HE SUCCUMBED TO SERIOUS ILLNESS

Now I ask Him to heal me, and He doesn't. I do not understand."

Days passed and fellow students and faculty continued to visit their beloved Sammy. One day as some of his friends gathered in his hospital room, they noticed the puzzled look was gone. His face was relaxed with a glowing peace.

"I understand now why my Father has not healed me. He showed me that I have finished my work here on earth. I have done all that I was meant to do. It is time for me to go and be with Him. I saw the angels! They will be coming for me soon!"

Dr. Reade came to sit with him. As Sammy related his latest conversation with his Father, Dr. Reade protested.

"But what about going back to Africa? What about your work with the children?"

Sammy smiled at his friend. "It is not my work, Dr. Reade. It is His. I have finished my job. He will

"I HAVE FINISHED MY WORK HERE ON EARTH"

send others better than I to do the work in Africa."

Dr. Reade's eyes brimmed with tears. "But Sammy—" His voice broke.

"I am so happy to be going home!" exclaimed Sammy.

The college president gazed at the young man who did not once complain of his suffering. "Sammy, are you afraid of death?"

Sammy laughed and shook his head. "How can I fear death? I have Jesus! Death is my friend!"

What a contrast to the terror death held for the young Kaboo who lay dying in Africa five years before! Kaboo had learned that death was the gateway to life. He understood that life was a bright eternal river that flowed from the throne of his Father.

Dr. Reade remembered when Sammy had come to him one day, laughing. He remembered his words. "Dr. Reade, I doubt I could possibly love my teachers in

"HOW CAN I FEAR DEATH? I HAVE JESUS!"

heaven more than I love you, and Dr. Stemen, and the rest of my teachers here." His eyes had twinkled in merriment. "But in heaven, I will not be so slow a student. I will be a fast learner there!"

The college president left Sammy to rest. He wondered if Sammy was right about dying. Everyone else seemed to think he would recover.

On May 12, 1893, Sammy stood at the window of his hospital room. It was a sunny spring day. He watched as Dr. Stemen, who lived across the street from the hospital, mowed his lawn.

"Dr. Stemen!" called Sammy from his window. "Don't work too hard!"

Dr. Stemen waved to his friend. Sammy returned to his chair.

In a matter of minutes, a nurse from the hospital frantically summoned Dr. Stemen to Sammy's room. She couldn't get the patient to respond to her.

Dr. Stemen took the ebony arm in his hand and felt

"DR. STEMEN... DON'T WORK TOO HARD!"

for a pulse. There was none. He looked at Sammy's face. It radiated joyful peace.

"He's gone," said the doctor softly.

Perhaps, echoing in the walls of that room were words from Sammy's favorite chapter in Scripture: "Do not let your hearts be troubled. Trust in God, trust also in me. In my Father's house are many rooms; if it were not so, I would have told you. I am going there to prepare a place for you.... I will come back and take you to be with me that you may be where I am." Sammy was in his Father's house!

The news of Samuel Morris' death swept across the university campus, dealing every heart a jolting blow. How could this be? He was so young, so full of promise. What a mighty ministry he was going to have! Why did the Lord allow him to die? What about the children in Liberia? What about the hundreds of people in the surrounding community who had come to love Sammy? These questions and the

"HE'S GONE"

swirling waves of grief swept through the believers at Taylor University.

The day of the funeral, the students carried Sammy's coffin in procession to his church on Berry Street. The streets and sidewalks of Fort Wayne were crowded with people. The church was filled to overflowing. At the Lindenwood Cemetery, mourners from all over the city came to say farewell to Samuel Morris.

After the funeral, the college students gathered in prayer meeting. They talked together of their beloved friend. One by one, three young men rose to their feet to declare that they felt the call of God to go to Africa in Sammy's place. This stirring of the missionary spirit on the Taylor University campus proved to be a lasting one.

After overcoming the initial shock of Sammy's death, his friends began to realize the greater vision that God had for his young life. God's measurement

STUDENTS CARRIED SAMMY'S COFFIN

of life is so different from people's measurements. It's not the length of a life that matters. Rather it is whether or not the life was lived wholeheartedly for the Lord. Sammy's simple faith in his Father caused others to be drawn to the Lord. His fervent prayers sparked intercession in those who heard him pray. His gentleness and willingness to serve humbled those around him, spurring them to be servants as well.

Sammy always pointed people to Jesus. When his reputation as a servant of the Lord spread, many people wrote to Taylor University requesting photographs of the inspiring young man. Sammy's reaction could be the theme of his life: "How I wish I could send them a picture of Jesus!"

In a way, Sammy's cry was answered. Because of his humility, his faith, and his love, his life was indeed a picture of Jesus. When God reached out to a young boy dying on a cross in Africa, it was the

SAMMY ALWAYS POINTED PEOPLE TO JESUS

beginning of a journey which would ultimately affect people around the world. What a testimony to the love and grace of God! Kaboo could have simply died of his wounds, alone and unknown. But God had a plan for his young life. He called him out of his misery and showered him with love.

Sammy's story is a miracle, a wonder. But it is a wonder and a marvel that any of us are saved. It is a miracle of grace when we hear the voice of God in His Gospel and follow that voice, set free from the clutching jungle of sin and the evil chieftain of the kingdom of darkness, Satan.

Prince Kaboo was torn from his family. He lost his earthly father. But God reached down and became a Father to him, a Father who would never leave or forsake His child. This wonderful Savior redeemed the pawn from death. And Sammy's response to such love provided a channel of giving that helped to change the lives of countless others.

GOD HAD A PLAN FOR HIS YOUNG LIFE

SAMUEL MORRIS

What did Sammy know that resulted in such far-reaching fruitfulness? He knew how much God loved the world. And he was fully convinced of the love of God for one boy named Kaboo.

HE KNEW HOW MUCH GOD LOVED THE WORLD

"I'M A FRIEND OF SAMUEL MORRIS"

In New York, several years after Sammy's death, the captain of a tramp vessel knocked on Stephen Merritt's door.

"Excuse me, sir," he said. "I'm a friend of Samuel Morris. My crew and I are anxious to hear about him. Can you tell me, is he well? How is he doing?"

Stephen Merritt looked into the grizzly face of the old captain. There was so much to tell of Sammy. Where to begin? When Merritt told him the news of Sammy's death, the captain fell silent. Overwhelmed with grief, he couldn't speak.

Stephen sat with him in the silence, sharing his grief. When at last he spoke, the captain testified to the wonderful influence Sammy had had on the entire crew.

"My men are from all parts of the world. We're all different, all from different cultures. Sammy did the impossible. Through his prayers, his singing, his way of living, he made us one. Where there was hate and division, there is now unity. We are like a family now."

Just as the lives of the captain and his men were forever changed by God through Sammy, Stephen Merritt's life was changed as well. He resolutely endeavored to walk with the Holy Spirit, following His leadership. His ministry exploded with fruitfulness. His prayers were powerful. Thousands of people came to Christ through his ministry.

When God is at work, the fruit lasts. As was the custom in those days, Sammy had been buried in the section of the cemetery reserved for African Americans. Because Sammy pulled down barriers between the races, his grave was moved to link the two sections, black and white, together. Thirty-five years after his death, a monument was erected to honor him. These words were carved in it:

"HE MADE US ONE"

SAMUEL MORRIS

Samuel Morris, 1873-1893
Prince Kaboo
Native of West Africa
Famous Christian Mystic
Apostle of Simple Faith
Exponent of the Spirit-filled Life

Sammy's grave site is visited more often by more people than any other grave in the cemetery. People have gone there and been drawn to pray and seek the Lord. Even in death, Samuel Morris still points people to Christ. One woman had gone to the cemetery to mourn the death of her husband. She was ill herself, alone, and without hope. She noticed a group of people gathering at the grave of Samuel Morris. She joined them. The testimony of his life gave her hope. She cried out to God. The woman left the cemetery, no longer alone. She walked out with her heavenly Father!

SHE WALKED OUT WITH HER HEAVENLY FATHER!

SAMUEL MORRIS

In 1896, Dr. Reade published a booklet scanning the life of Prince Kaboo. In it he observed: "Samuel Morris was a divinely-sent messenger of God to touch Taylor University. He thought he was coming over to prepare himself for his mission in the world— he was coming over to this country to prepare Taylor University for her mission in this world. She was ready for his message, and it lifted her to a new realm. She got a vision of the world's needs. It was no longer local, neither national, but world-wide.... Since then the students have been going to the ends of the world."

Sammy's impact on Taylor University is still felt today. Taylor is a thriving college that continues to send out students as missionaries around the globe.

AFTERWORD

The legacy of Samuel Morris—Prince Kaboo lives on. His testimony and his child-like faith inspire people to this day. Sammy would be the first to say that it is not his personality that can so engage the human spirit, rather it is the Holy Spirit of God working through him. It is a testimony to what God can do with the life of one who follows Jesus wholeheartedly.

BIBLIOGRAPHY

ANGEL IN EBONY. (video) Gospel Films, Inc.

Baldwin, Lindley. SAMUEL MORRIS. Minneapolis, Minnesota: Bethany House Publishers, 1942.

Evans, A.R. SAMMY MORRIS. Grand Rapids, Michigan: Zondervan Publishing House, 1958.

Reade, Reverend T.C. SAMUEL MORRIS (PRINCE KABOO). Upland, Indiana: Taylor University Press, 1896.

Warner, Esther. NEW SONG IN A STRANGE LAND. Boston: Houghton Mifflin Company, 1948.

Wengatz, John C. SAMMY MORRIS—THE SPIRIT-FILLED LIFE. Upland, Indiana: Taylor University Press, 1954.

THUNDER IN THE VALLEY

DRAMA! ADVENTURE! ACTION!

AT A BOOKSTORE NEAR YOU!

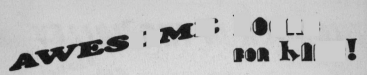